# How to Determine the Replacement Cost of Equipment

## A Step by Step Guide

I0462849

### By Meir Liraz

Published by BizMove
www.bizmove.com

ISBN: 9781090239068

# Table of Contents

MEIR LIRAZ

# 1. Introduction

The decision to replace a piece of equipment should be based on facts and figures. The judgment which the owner-manager of a small company makes should be the result of weighing the costs of keeping the old equipment against the cost of its replacement.

This guide discusses the elements involved in making such a cost comparison. Examples are used to illustrate the gathering and use of the appropriate cost figures.

Sooner or later, you must decide whether you should keep an existing unit of equipment or replace it with a new unit. As time goes by, equipment deteriorates and becomes obsolete. Frequent breakdowns occur, defective output increases, unit labor costs rise, and production schedules cannot be met. At some point, these occurrences become serious enough to cause you to wonder whether or not you should replace the equipment.

The problem is that the new equipment costs money, and the question that comes to you is: Will the advantages of the new equipment be great enough to justify the investment it requires?

You answer this question by making a cost comparison.

To recognize the better alternative you need to know the total cost of each alternative - keeping the old equipment or buying a replacement. Once these costs are determined, you can compare them and identify the more economical equipment. The paragraphs that follow discuss the individual costs which you must consider when computing the total cost of the old and new equipment.

## 2. Depreciation

One of the costs connected with any type of equipment is depreciation. For cost comparison purposes, depreciation is simply the amount by which an asset decreases in value over some period of time. For example, if you bought a piece of equipment for $20,000 and sold it for $6,000 after seven years of service, you would say that the depreciation during the seven-year period was $20,000 minus $6,000, or $14,000. This $14,000 was one of your costs of owning the equipment for that period.

From this, it follows that when considering equipment replacement, you must calculate the future depreciation expense that you will experience with both the old and the new equipment.

Insofar as the new equipment is concerned, this calls for knowing certain things about the equipment. You need to know (1) its first cost, (2) its estimated service life, and (3) its expected salvage value. The difference between the first cost and the salvage value will represent the amount by which the equipment will depreciate during its life - that is, during the time you expect to use it.

You determine the depreciation expense for the old equipment in the same general way but for one import difference. The difference is that no expenditure is required to procure the equipment because you already own it. However, a decision to keep it does require an investment at the present time. This investment is equal to the asset's market value - that is, to the amount of money the asset would bring in if it were replaced and sold. If this amount is not equal to the equipment's book value. the depreciation expense that was shown for accounting purposes is in error because it did not reflect the actual depreciation.

So to determine the actual future depreciation expense that will be experienced with the old equipment, you must know (1) its present market value, (2) its estimated remaining service life, and (3) its expected salvage value at the end of that life. The difference between the present market value and the future salvage value represents the amount by which the equipment will depreciate during its remaining life in your business.

To sum up, you must begin your cost comparison by determining the first cost of the new equipment and estimating its service life and salvage value.

Also, you must determine the market value of the old equipment and estimate its remaining service life and future salvage value.

# 3. Interest

In addition to depreciation, every piece of equipment generates an interest expense. This expense occurs because owning an asset ties up some of your capital. If you had to borrow this capital you would have to pay for the use of the money. This "out-of-pocket" cost is one of the costs of owning the equipment.

The story is the same even when you use your own money. In this case, the amount involved is no longer available for other investments which could bring you a return. This "opportunity cost" is one of the costs of owning the equipment.

To cite an example, suppose that the market value of an asset during a given year is $10,000. Suppose also that at the same time, you are getting capital at a cost of 15 percent per year. On the other hand, suppose that if you converted the asset into cash, you could invest the money and realize a rate of return of 15 percent per year. In either case, a decision to own that asset during that year would be costing you 15 percent of $10,000, or $1,500 in interest.

Thus, in any comparison of equipment alternatives,

you must take the cost of money into account. So, when determining whether or not existing equipment should be replaced, you must estimate what money is costing you in terms of a percent per year.

# 4. Operating Costs

There is a third type of cost - the cost of operation - that is experienced with a piece of equipment. Typical operating cost are expenditures for labor, materials, supervision, maintenance, and power.

These cost must be considered because your choice of equipment affects them. You may find it convenient to estimate these costs on an annual basis. You can get figures for each unit of equipment by estimating its next-year operating costs as well as the annual rate at which these costs are likely to increase as wage rates rise and the equipment deteriorates.

For example, you might say that operating cost for the new equipment are likely to be $16,000 during the first year of its life. You might also estimate that after the first year, the operating costs will increase at a rate of $500 a year.

You can simplify the problem of estimating these costs by either (1) ignoring those costs that are the same for the old and the new equipment or (2) estimating only the differences between the operating costs of the two units. With this simplification, the total costs which you calculate for each type of equipment will be understated by the same amount. Therefore, the difference between these total costs will remain the same, and you will still be able to recognize the more economical alternative.

## 5. Revenues

Often, the revenues generated by the old and the new equipment will be the same. When this is true, revenues can be ignored for the same reason that you can ignore equal operating costs.

But if revenues are affected by the choice of equipment, they must be considered. For example, you might estimate that the higher quality of output from the new equipment will increase annual sales by $1,200. You can handle this difference in revenues in either of two ways.

One way is to show the $1,200 as an additional annual cost that will be experienced with the old equipment.

The other way is to treat the $1,200 as a negative annual cost and associate it with the new equipment. The total cost which you calculate will be affected by your choice of method, but the difference between these cost will remain the same.

## 6. An Annual Average Cost

In brief, you can make the necessary cost analysis on the new and old equipment only after you have the proper data for each. For the new equipment, the data include first cost, service life, salvage value, operating costs, and revenue advantage. For the old equipment, the data include market value, remaining service life, future salvage value, and operating costs. In addition, for both alternatives, the cost of money must be stated in the form of an interest rate.

By using these data, you can determine the elements of the total costs. These elements consist of depreciation expense, interest expense, operating costs, and possibly lost revenues. Now, it so happens that these costs can be expressed in a variety of ways.

However, the simplest way for cost comparison purposes is to describe these cost elements in terms of an average annual cost. Doing so permits you to calculate and compare the total average annual costs of the old and new equipment and reach a decision.

How these costs can be computed is shown in the example that follows.

## 7. The Old Equipment

Look first at some facts about an old piece of equipment. It has a market value of $7,000. If retained, its service life is expected to be four years, and its salvage value is expected to be $1,000. Next-year operating costs are estimated to be $8,000 but will probably increase at an annual rate of $200. The cost of money is 12 percent per year. With this set of figures, you can obtain the total average annual cost of the alternative of keeping this equipment.

**Annual Depreciation Expense.** You begin by calculating the equipment's average annual depreciation expense. You do this by determining the total depreciation and dividing that amount by the asset's four-year life. Your answer is $1,500 which you get as follows:

Annual depreciation =

$$\frac{\$7,000 - \$1,000}{4} = \$1,500$$

**Annual Interest Expense.** Next, you calculate the average annual interest expense. The maximum investment in the equipment is $7,000, its present market value. But as time goes by, the investment in the asset decreases because its market value decreases. The minimum investment is reached at the end of the equipment's life when it has a salvage value of $1,000. The average investment will be the average of these maximum and minimum values. You calculate it as follows:

Average investment =

$$\frac{\$7,000 + \$1,000}{2} = \$4,000$$

To determine the average annual interest expense, you multiply the average investment ($4,000, in this example) by the annual interest rate of 12 percent. Doing so yields:

Annual Interest = $4,000 x .12 = $480

**Annual Operating Costs.** You can determine the average annual operating costs by computing the average of the individual annual operating costs. In this example, they are estimated to be $8,000, $8,200, $8,400, and $8,600. The average for these figures is $8,300 which you obtain as follows:

Annual operating costs =

$$\frac{\$8,000 + \$8,200 + \$8,400 + \$8,600}{4} = \$8,300$$

**Total Average Annual Cost.** For the old equipment, the total average annual cost is simply the sum of the calculated average annual cost for: (1) depreciation, (2) interest, and (3) operating expenses. This sum is $10,280, as shown below.

| Item | Average annual cost |
|---|---|
| Depreciation | $1,500 |
| Interest | 480 |
| Operating Costs | 8,300 |
| | |
| Total | $10,280 |

# 8. The New Equipment

Look now at the facts on a piece of new equipment which may be a replacement for the old equipment. The first cost of this new equipment is $30,000. Its life is estimated to be ten years, and it will probably have a salvage value of $6,000. Operating costs with this equipment are expected to average $5,200 a year. Furthermore, it is estimated to have an annual revenue advantage of $300 over the old equipment. The cost of money is 12 percent per year.

You use the same approach as you did for the old equipment to determine the total average annual cost of this new equipment.

**Annual Depreciation Expense.** You start with the average annual depreciation expense and find it to be $2,400, as follows:

Annual depreciation =

$$\frac{\$30,000 - \$6,000}{10} = \$2,400$$

**Annual Interest Expense.** You multiply the average investment in this asset by the interest rate to obtain the average annual interest expense. The average investment is $18,000 (one-half of the sum of the $30,000 first cost and the $6,000 salvage value). The average annual interest expense is $2,160 obtained as follows:

Annual interest = .5 ($30,000 + $6,000) x.12 = $2,160

**Total Average Annual Cost.** When you also take the estimated operating costs and revenue advantage into account, you find the total average annual cost to be $9,460, as shown below.

| Item | Average annual cost |
| --- | --- |
| Depreciation | $2,400 |
| Interest | 2,160 |
| Operating Costs | 5,200 |
| | $9,760 |
| Less: Revenue advantage | 300 |
| | $9,460 |

# 9. The Comparison

When you have the total average annual cost for the old and the new equipment, you are ready to compare the two. In the example, the calculated annual cost is $10,280 for the old equipment and $9,460 for the new. On the surface, the new equipment is more economical than the old. But is it?

You may argue that with the old equipment you are committing yourself for only four years, whereas with the new, your commitment is for ten years. This fact suggests a need for considering the kind of equipment that may be available for replacement purposes four years from now as compared with ten years from now.

But no one can forecast that far into the future. It is best to ignore the nature of future replacements in your computations and assume that the replacement available four years from now will have the same annual cost as the one available ten years from now.

## 10. Irreducible Factors

When your calculated annual costs show that the one unit of equipment has a decided advantage over the other, you can usually select the better alternative by comparing these calculated costs. But what do you do when the annual costs of the old and the new equipment do not differ greatly? In such a case, you should consider the fact that the estimates might contain errors and that there are things on which a dollar value cannot be placed.

So you may have to base your decision on irreducible factors - factors that cannot be reduced to dollars and cents.

A few examples will suggest the nature of such factors.

First, if total average annual costs are about the same, you will probably favor the equipment that required the smaller investment and has the shorter life. The same will hold true when you suspect that technological advances will result in more efficient equipment becoming available in the near future.

As another example, you will prefer the equipment which has greater output capacity, safety, and reliability even though the value of these is unknown.

And finally, when you suspect that interest rates and the price of new equipment will increase significantly, you will be inclined to invest in new equipment now rather than later.

MEIR LIRAZ

MEIR LIRAZ